AFRICA

Jill Lewis

CELEBRATION PRESS
Pearson Learning Group

Map of the World

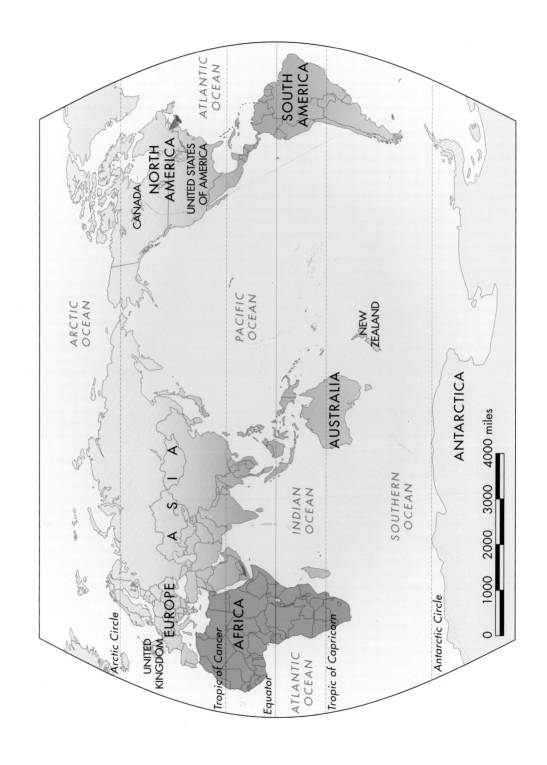

ARCTIC OCEAN

Arctic Circle

UNITED KINGDOM

EUROPE

CANADA

NORTH AMERICA

UNITED STATES OF AMERICA

ATLANTIC OCEAN

SOUTH AMERICA

A S I A

AFRICA

Tropic of Cancer

Equator

ATLANTIC OCEAN

Tropic of Capricorn

PACIFIC OCEAN

INDIAN OCEAN

NEW ZEALAND

AUSTRALIA

SOUTHERN OCEAN

Antarctic Circle

ANTARCTICA

0   1000   2000   3000   4000 miles

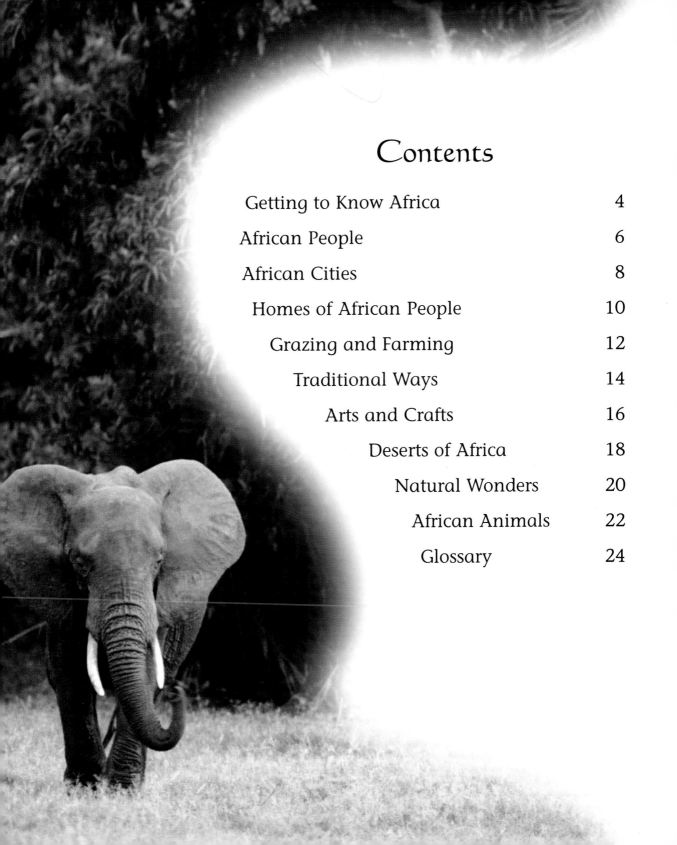

Contents

Getting to Know Africa

Africa is the second largest continent in the world. It has fifty-three countries, including the islands of Madagascar, Mauritius, and the Seychelles. The largest country is Sudan and the smallest is the Seychelles. The Seychelles is actually a group of islands.

A beach at La Digne, which is an island in the Seychelles group of islands.

Buyers and sellers at an animal market in Sudan.

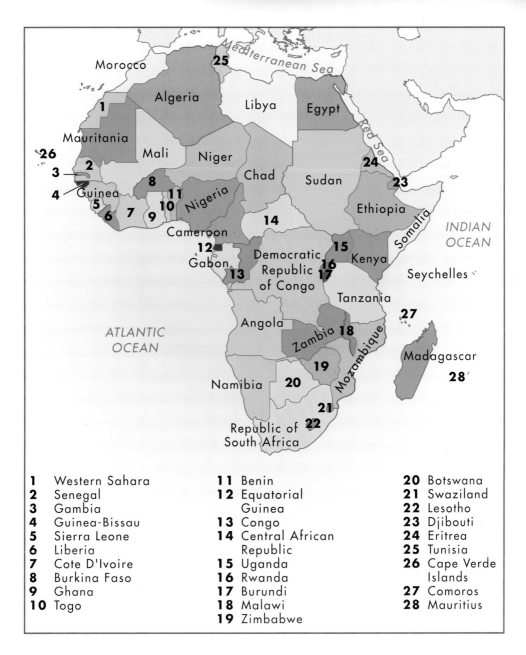

1	Western Sahara	**11**	Benin	**20**	Botswana
2	Senegal	**12**	Equatorial	**21**	Swaziland
3	Gambia		Guinea	**22**	Lesotho
4	Guinea-Bissau	**13**	Congo	**23**	Djibouti
5	Sierra Leone	**14**	Central African	**24**	Eritrea
6	Liberia		Republic	**25**	Tunisia
7	Cote D'Ivoire	**15**	Uganda	**26**	Cape Verde
8	Burkina Faso	**16**	Rwanda		Islands
9	Ghana	**17**	Burundi	**27**	Comoros
10	Togo	**18**	Malawi	**28**	Mauritius
		19	Zimbabwe		

Africa

African People

The population of Africa is 840 million people. There are more than 800 ethnic groups. Each group has its own language, culture, and unique way of life.

The Tuareg people live in the Sahara.

The Zulu people live in southeastern Africa.

This woman comes from the town of Djenne in Mali, West Africa.

Masai dancers in central Kenya

African Cities

In the cities, there are hospitals, schools, marketplaces, beautiful houses of worship, museums, and art galleries. Many people move from rural areas to the cities to find work. The cities are often overcrowded and polluted.

Cairo, capital city of Egypt

City square in Marrakesh, Morocco

Capetown, capital city of the Republic of South Africa

Homes of African People

Many homes in rural areas do not have running water, telephones, or electricity. In some houses, there may be only one room where all the family members live. Often there are no schools, so the children learn at home.

These traditional houses have very small windows and very thick walls made from mud brick.

Tents of the Berber people, in the Sahara, Morocco

A Somali nomad sets up an "aqal"—a wood-framed portable hut

Grazing and Farming

Nearly two-thirds of Africans live by farming the land or by keeping goats, sheep, and cattle.

The main crops of northern Africa include wheat, rice, barley, oranges, dates, and cotton.

In central Africa, corn, sweet potatoes, yams, bananas, cocoa, tea, coffee, and cotton are important.

The main crops of southern Africa include vegetables, corn, fruit, peanuts, coffee, tobacco, tea, and sugar.

Picking cotton in Zimbabwe

Coffee beans growing in Kenya

Masai herdsman,
with his cattle,
Tanzania

Goats feeding in
a tree, Morocco

Traditional Ways

Many African people follow the traditional ways of their ancestors. They take part in festivals such as a celebration of the first rains or harvest time.

Pokot tribeswoman in traditional dress, Kenya

Zulu village chief in traditional dress, South Africa

Ndebele woman in traditional dress, South Africa

These traditional masks are made from wood. These men belong to the Dogon tribe of Mali. The Dogons wear masks when they dance at ceremonies.

There are many special traditions, ceremonies, and costumes linked to the different African ethnic groups and religions.

Arts and Crafts

African artists create unique paintings, statues, masks, jewelry, musical instruments, pottery, and fabrics.

Rock painting of elephants, South Africa

Adinkra is hand-painted cloth. The Asante people of Ghana are known for their unique art of adinkra printing.

The Kuba tribe lives in Zaire. This Kuba tribesman is carving a small wooden figure.

Deserts of Africa

The Sahara takes up most of northern Africa. Some northern Africans live in the Sahara as nomads.

The Kalahari Desert is covered with reddish sand. It lies mainly in the countries of Botswana, Namibia, and South Africa. The people who live in this desert are mostly nomads. Many animals and birds live in the Kalahari.

The Namib Desert, in southwest Africa, is one of the hottest and driest places on Earth. Many animals such as gemsbok, ostriches, warthogs, scorpions, geckos, and spiders live in the Namib.

Deserts of Africa

The Sahara is the world's largest desert.

An oasis is a fertile place in the desert where water can be found.

Natural Wonders

The Nile River is 4,132 miles long. It is the world's longest river. It flows through Egypt into the Mediterranean Sea. The Nile Valley is very fertile and a lot of people live there. This area was the site of an ancient Egyptian civilization. It is the home of the Great Pyramids.

Victoria Falls, on the Zambesi River between Zambia and Zimbabwe, is a spectacular waterfall. It is Africa's most popular attraction. The African name for Victoria Falls is *Mosi-oa-tunya*, which means "smoke that thunders."

Victoria Falls, Zimbabwe

Banks of the
Nile River, Egypt

Mount Kilimanjaro,
Tanzania

The highest mountain in Africa is Mount Kilimanjaro in
Tanzania. It is 19,340 feet high. Although Mount Kilimanjaro
is situated near the equator, in the hottest part of the world,
Mount Kilimanjaro is always capped with snow.

African Animals

Africa is home to thousands of species of mammals, birds, insects, fish, reptiles, and amphibians.

If you went on a safari to one of the national parks, you would see herds of animals, such as antelopes, gazelles, zebras, and buffaloes. Animals such as lions, leopards, and cheetahs prey on these herds.

Leopards roam parts of Africa.

Hippopotamuses wallow in rivers.

This African lake is home to flocks of flamingos.

Many of Africa's creatures are endangered. Too much hunting, the destruction of the natural environment, and changes in climate have threatened many animals.

The world environment movement is helping African countries to preserve their wildlife.

Glossary

ancestor	a much older person in the family line, no longer living, such as a great-grandfather
ancient	very old
capped	topped
civilization	human culture and society
continent	one of the main land masses of the world
culture	a way of living
endangered	in danger of being killed so that none are left
ethnic	relating to the culture of a group of people
farming	growing crops or raising animals on a farm
fertile	land where there is water and good soil
gallery	a covered area where objects, such as paintings, are placed for viewing
nomad	person who moves from place to place, for example in a desert, looking for food and water
polluted	become unclean or dirty
population	the total number of persons living in a place
preserve	keep safe from harm
running water	water flowing through pipes to a tap
spectacular	amazing, thrilling
threatened	cause danger to
traditional	related to the customs of ancestors
unique	something of which there is only one